REVOLVERS

T&J

Published by TAJ Books International LLC 2014
5501 Kincross Lane, Charlotte
North Carolina, USA
28277

www.tajbooks.com
www.tajminibooks.com

Copyright © 2014 TAJ Books International LLC

All rights reserved. No part of this publication may be reproduced, stored in a retrieval system, or transmitted in any form or by any means, electronic, mechanical, photocopying, recording, or otherwise, without the prior written permission of the Publisher and copyright holders.

All notations of errors or omissions (author inquiries, permissions) concerning the content of this book should be addressed to info@tajbooks.com.

The Publisher wishes to thank all image contributors. The Publisher believes the use of the images at the size depicted qualifies as fair use under United States copyright law.

ISBN 978-1-84406-340-6 Hardcover
978-1-62732-006-1 Paperback

Printed in China

1 2 3 4 5 18 17 16 15 14

REVOLVERS

T&J

RICK SAPP

REVOLVERS

The days when a town constable carried a simple cudgel and could unceremoniously toss a man or woman into the stocks are long gone in America. Colonial America enjoyed relatively little crime, with most "crimes" being offenses against established custom rather than murder or theft, so a sheriff could get away with only carrying a stick to bash the occasional stubborn head.

A peace officer in the budding United States was rarely confronted by a violent or unpredictable person, but this began to change as wealth aggregated and cities grew. Officers could carry a flintlock pistol, but it was a one-shot weapon, certainly deadly enough, but if additional firepower was needed, he of necessity gathered a posse.

Soldiers, too, and even hunters found the flintlock musket to be adequate within 100 yards, but otherwise limited. Flintlocks were heavy, and the supporting gear—the flints and powder horns of the 18th and 19th centuries—was cumbersome. For top performance, they required continuous attention in the field and firing a shot resulted in a billowing cloud of smoke from the black powder, eliminating any possibility that the shooter's position would remain concealed.

Equipping one-shot firearms with bayonets was a necessary throwback to the days of the pike and halberd. Troops fired in volleys and then charged the enemy with fixed bayonets. Eventually, a few pistols were also equipped with under-barrel bayonets, but their use in a fight must have been extremely awkward.

Evolution, whether biological or mechanical, is a tedious and mysterious process, especially when trying to piece together a story line from the historical record. It is easy to imagine that firearms changed magically, inevitably, step by step, from the days of the flintlock to those of the high power revolver, but upon closer inspection we know that could not be the case. In fact, the first efforts to create a gun that fired multiple times were based on the flintlock model.

Collier's Big Step. Around the world, many men have been intrigued by the concept of a gun that fired more than one time, accurately and reliably. Experiments and ideas must have been endless as private individuals and government contractors experimented with hundreds of designs including superposed loads.

An almost forgotten Boston inventor and gunsmith named Elisha Collier may have been the first person to build a true handgun with revolving cylinder. Collier was a member of the "in-between" generation, born after the War for Independence and dying prior to the Civil War.

In that era, Collier's tools were flintlock muskets, a mechanical ability, and a restless curiosity. He probably experimented with multi-barrel pepperboxes at first, those multi-barrel, multi-chamber handguns that were neither especially accurate beyond a few yards nor entirely reliable.

Mechanical sophistication 200 years ago had advanced far beyond the stone-stuck-upon-stone stage, but was nowhere near the capability of mass production in which part designs necessarily became increasingly precise. Every aspect of a barrel, grip, and cylinder that Collier built was handcrafted. Nothing was truly interchangeable, and depending upon natural flints to reliably produce a proper spark worked well only in the general instance, especially with the primitive black powder of the day.

Collier's single-action flintlock-based patent was issued in 1818 and included a revolutionary self-priming action. When the hammer was cocked a compartment automatically released gunpowder into the pan. Disregarding the complex designs of the pepperboxes, Collier relied on a single barrel and a conventional spring-based mechanical action for decreased weight, increased accuracy, and faster reloads.

The Bostonian's designs, including those for shotguns and carbines, were not widely accepted in the U.S. In England however, his flintlock revolvers were mass produced by John Evans & Son of London and used in quantity by the British army in India. Between 1819 and 1824, more than 10,000 of Collier's early revolvers were manufactured.

Flintlock to Percussion Cap. The muzzleloading flintlock seems extraordinarily primitive today, but in its time it was a major advancement. Flintlocks after all did not require the matchlock's continuously burning cord and, compared to the wheel-lock, the action was relatively simple and the cost of production was modest. Flintlocks proved themselves as infantry weapons for 200 years or more and are still used by period reenactors and hunters who prefer a more nuanced weapon than, for instance, a semi-automatic modern sporting rifle.

The cap-lock or percussion cap system, which relied on an encapsulated chemical primer, followed the flintlock in firearms development. It was a tremendous advance, allowing a gun to be fired in wet weather, but the "shelf-life" of the percussion cap system was barely a half century.

Perhaps tiring of never-ending efforts to keep his powder dry in England's blustery, dreary weather, a Scottish preacher and waterfowl hunter named Alexander Forsyth developed the first cap-lock system in 1807. He filled a tiny bottle with fulminate of mercury, an explosive preparation that is extremely sensitive to shock, discarded the flint, and drilled a hole in the barrel to hold the burning fulminate of mercury, which led directly to the powder.

Forsyth must have been one of many

men working independently to develop a better ignition system for firearms. Still, a generation passed before an updated version of Forsyth's controlled-powder-ignition idea was universally accepted.

Generally, the process of evolution builds toward increasing complexity, but revolvers evolved otherwise toward a simpler, albeit more mechanically sophisticated, system: wheel-lock to flintlock to cap-lock to breech-loading. A 19th-century gunsmith could convert a flintlock musket or rifle to use percussion-cap ignition by making only minor alterations to the action. The percussion cap replaced the flint, the steel "frizzen," and the powder pan of the flint-lock mechanism.

In flintlock design, the flint was held in place by a cocking arm or hammer called a "cock." In cap-lock design, the hammer now had full- and half-cock positions. The safe half-cock setting allowed a shooter to place the explosive cap on the nipple without fearing that it would explode in his hand. After pulling the hammer back to full cock, he pulled the trigger to release the hammer which then struck the cap, crushing it against the nipple and sending a jet of fire down through the hollow tube in the nipple, a more modern version of the matchlock touch-hole. The stream of fire ignited the powder charge in the barrel and the spent cap generally fell off when the hammer was again moved back to the half-cock position for reloading.

The "modern" percussion cap was effectively invented by an Englishman in 1814 (though others also claimed that achievement), in that age when a man might be a famous painter and a mechanical inventor as well. The artist Joshua Shaw designed a tiny copper cup and filled it with a mixture of fulminate of mercury, chlorate of potash, and ground glass. This was a significant enhancement over former designs. Because the English clergyman Forsyth threatened legal action, Shaw kept his invention a secret until he could move to America and procure a patent in 1822. By the 1830s, the British, French, and Russian armies began adopting Shaw's ignition system.

Father of the Revolver. The "first" of anything is often disputed, especially dealing with dates and events that are poorly documented. We give the son of a Connecticut farmer, one Samuel Colt, however, credit for inventing the first working percussion revolver and almost no one questions the honor.

Sam Colt spent the year 1832 at sea, aboard the two-masted sailing ship *Corvo*. He was 18 years old and sailed to Calcutta, India, and back. The story he later told was that he became fascinated by the action of the ship's wheel as it spun and synchronized with the clutch, thus controlling the ship's directional movement. A separate version suggests that he watched the capstan, a rotating wheel used to control lines to sails and spars, and to redirect the force of the wind. These

Samuel Colt
"God made man, but Samuel Colt made them equal."

devices, according to Colt, gave him the idea for spinning or rotating chambers that held ammunition. While aboard the brig he even carved a realistic model of a revolver out of scrap wood.

In reality, Colt may also have seen—they were fairly common in India—one of Elisha Collier's flintlock revolvers and simply adapted that technology with his own inventive refinements to the newer percussion-cap ignition system. Colt's enhancement rotated the cylinder by the action of cocking the hammer, which activated a spring-powered pawl. The pawl then locked the cylinder in place. The cylinders of 1830s smoothbore pepperbox revolvers were still rotated by hand without standardized mechanical indexing or alignment, which came later, and resulted in the rifled-bore "transitional revolver" of the 1850s.

Just as today, the first thing successful inventors thought of was a patent to protect their ideas. In 1835, Colt traveled to England and France to patent his revolver schematics. He was only 21 years old. Then he returned to the U.S. for a patent ... and began raising money.

With patents, working models, and a personal investment, Colt incorporated as the Patent Arms Manufacturing Company. In a Paterson, New Jersey, factory he began turning out revolving cylinder handguns, rifles, and even shotguns.

The initial investment fared poorly because even though the Paterson Colts were functional, they were neither efficient nor reliable. Following the cap-and-ball model, gunpowder and bullets were loaded into the front of the cylinders while the primer was inserted into a hollow nipple located on the outside of the cylinder where it would be struck by the hammer. But the era's black powders left a great deal of residue after a shot and this fouling hampered moving parts. Even though his Paterson guns were used in the Seminole War in Florida and in fighting to establish the Republic of Texas, the government lost interest and Colt was forced to close his factory.

After several famous Texas Rangers gave him their personal blessing, Colt tried again with greater attention to effective design of a six-cylinder handgun. This time the government bought his guns in quantity, notably the massive 4-pound, 9-ounce, .44-caliber Walker Colt, named after Captain Samuel Walker, Texas Rangers.

Colt's second production effort resulted in a modern factory in Hartford, Connecticut, for his Colt's Patent Fire-Arms Manufacturing Company. There, firearms were designed, molded, machined, fitted, stamped with a serial number, hardened, and assembled. Colt emphasized precision production and worked tirelessly to promote and sell his products. By 1851, the Hartford facility was turning out fresh firearms models to supply a national sense of unrest as well as the flood of immigrants moving west into the Louisiana Purchase and beyond, to California and Oregon. Colt even opened a factory in London. Within the decade, this self-taught farmer's son was considered one of the 10 wealthiest men in America.

A hard worker—some have called him a driven man—Sam Colt died on January 10, 1862. He was only 47 years old. By that time his Hartford Armory employed more than 1,000 men and was operating at full capacity, turning out cap-lock revolvers and other firearms for the Union's Civil War effort. In his lifetime he produced more than 400,000 guns and left behind an estate worth about $15 million, a monumental sum of money at that time.

Mr. Smith, Meet Mr. Wesson ... and Mr. Winchester. Horace Smith learned the firearms trade while working at the National Armory in Springfield, Massachusetts. Dan Wesson learned as an apprentice to his brother, Edwin, a leading maker of target rifles and pistols in the 1840s.

In 1852, Smith and Wesson formed a partnership in Norwich, Connecticut, intent on manufacturing a lever-action repeating pistol that could use a fully self-contained cartridge. It was not a radical idea, but it was a significant departure from the cap-lock system. Unfortunately, within two years, their business, the Volcanic Repeating Arms Co., was on the verge of failure, and they sold to Oliver Winchester who named his new company after himself.

A dozen years later, using the original lever-action design created by Smith and Wesson, Winchester's company emerged as the famous Winchester Repeating Arms.

Rollin White is credited with inventing a revolver—or at least patenting the design in 1855—with a bored-through cylinder that allowed cartridges to be loaded from the rear. At first, Sam Colt dismissed the idea as a novelty and White filed his patent independently. The next year, he licensed the popular idea to Smith and Wesson, but even after the patent expired in 1869 White was involved in patent infringement lawsuits.

In 1857, Smith and Wesson made a second attempt to manufacture a small revolver to fire the self-contained rimfire cartridge they patented in August 1854. Their patented revolver fired a .22 Short with four grains of black powder behind a conical bullet. This first successful cartridge revolver put Smith and Wesson on the map.

Civil War Opportunities. The U.S. Civil War was devastating to the nation's social fabric, but northern factories that turned out firearms prospered. Even Remington, one of America's oldest continuously operating corporate brands, known primarily for rifles and shotguns, gave revolvers a try.

Remington's 1858 New Model six-shot percussion revolver was manufactured in .36 (Navy) or .44 (Army) caliber. When the Colt factory burned (Confederate saboteurs were suspected) in 1864, halting production of the highly regarded 1861 Army and 1851 Navy designs, Remington became a substitute. The Model 1858 proved itself during the war and in the American West, in its original percussion configuration and later as a metallic cartridge conversion. The New Model was built with an innovative "top-strap" solid frame design that fully enclosed the cylinder. This made the handgun stronger and less wear-prone than the open-top Colt revolvers of the same era.

By the 1860s, most revolvers fired commercially made combustible cartridges, constructed of a paper envelope filled with powder and glued to the base of a conical bullet. The cartridge self-consumed on firing as did the beeswax cap, placed on top of the lead bullet to prevent cross-firing of black powder in other chambers. Combustible cartridges considerably sped up revolver loading, and hence firing, and use of high-performance sporting-grade black powder minimized fouling.

The Conversion Era and the SAA. Small developments sometimes lead to big changes: the Smith and Wesson rimfire cartridge and self-contained cartridges. It was only a matter of time before a self-contained metallic centerfire cartridge included a primer to close out the percussion cap era.

Meanwhile, Smith and Wesson realized that when the Rollin White patent expired they would need a new design to maintain their hard-won market position. In 1870 they began marketing the Model 3 American, a single-action, cartridge-firing, top-break revolver originally chambered in .44 caliber. The Model 3 was the first large-caliber cartridge revolver and built the Smith and Wesson reputation in handgun manufacturing. The two most important customers for the new revolver were the U.S. Cavalry, which purchased 1,000 units for use on the Western frontier, and the Imperial Government of Russia. The Model 3 was used by Wyatt Earp during the OK Corral Gunfight with the Clanton Gang.

In 1871, Colt employees Charles Richards and William Mason made their mark on revolver history by receiving a patent to convert percussion revolvers to breech loaders that fired self-contained cartridges. It was an instant success and led directly to the most famous sidearm of the Old West, the Single-Action Army.

No handgun defined ultimate closing of the American frontier as much as the Colt Single-Action Army, also known as the SAA or Peacemaker. It was the classic six-shooter, a single-action revolver originally designed for the U.S. government, and it served as the standard military service revolver until 1892.

With its bored-through revolver cylinders, the SAA was eventually offered in more than 30 calibers with various barrel lengths. Not until a generation had passed was the SAA replaced as the primary U.S. military sidearm by the .38 LC, Colt Model 1892, a double-action revolver with swing-out cylinder.

The Peacemaker was present everywhere. Custer's men of the 7th Cavalry carried them into battle at the Little Big Horn in 1876. Theodore Roosevelt's Rough Riders charged up San Juan Hill wielding the .45 caliber Artillery Model in 1898. George Patton carried a custom-made SAA with ivory grips engraved with his initials and an eagle. He used the gun during the Mexican Punitive Expedition of 1916 to kill two of Pancho Villa's lieutenants and carried it until his death in 1945.

The Colt SAA remains one of the most widely collected and recognized firearms in the world. When production ceased in 1940, as many as 310,386 guns (excluding the Flat Top and Bisley patterns) had been sold. Popular demand caused Colt to recommence manufacturing in 1955.

Single-Action, Double-Action. Revolver development was not limited to the U.S. though. British gunsmith Robert Adams patented the first successful double-action revolver in 1851. A single-action such as Colt's famous Peacemaker required the hammer to be cocked manually, usually with a thumb. Cocking advances the cylinder to the next round and locks the cylinder in place, aligning it with the barrel. When the trigger is pulled, it releases the hammer, which strikes the firing pin and fires the round in the chamber. To repeat fire, the hammer must be manually cocked again.

In double action, the trigger pull draws back the hammer while the cylinder is being indexed to the next round. As the trigger draws back it eventually releases the hammer to strike the firing pin. A cocking action separate from the trigger pull is unnecessary. Generally, the self-cocking double-action trigger pull is heavier that a single-action gun.

Many of today's handguns can be fired either single- or double-action. They are designated SA/DA. DAO indicates double-action-only.

Period Guns and Rise of the 1911. In the late 1800s Smith and Wesson introduced a line of hammerless revolvers. The company's .38 Military and Police, the Model 10, lays claim to be—after Colt's Peacemaker—one of the most famous revolvers in the world because of its reliability, durability, and modest price. The Model 10 has been in continual production since its introduction and has been used by practically every police agency and military force in the world.

Colt's Model 1889 was the first double-action revolver to use a swing-out cylinder, which was released by a sliding latch. The Colt design allowed for fast loading, but maintained the strength of a solid frame.

It took Smith and Wesson seven years to follow with the Model 10, or 1896 Hand Ejector. The design improved on Colt's 1889 gun with a combined center pin and ejector rod to lock the cylinder in position. The 1889 had lacked a center pin and was prone to move out of alignment. The six-shot double-action Smith and Wesson featured a cylinder release latch on the left side of the frame and eventually was produced in multiple barrel lengths. More than six million Model 10 handguns have been produced.

The English produced their own classic revolver, the Webley, a series of hinged frame or top-break centerfire revolvers, which Webley & Scott began producing in the 1870s. The Webleys, with their various upgrades and design modifications, were the standard issue service pistol for military and law enforcement for the British Empire from 1887 to 1963, an amazing design success of 76 years. Thus, the gun was known and recognized around the world. The powerful .455 Webley Mk I (retired only in 1947) featured automatic extraction; breaking the revolver open for reloading also operated the extractor, which automatically shoved spent cartridges out of the cylinder.

Belgian manufacturer Léon Nagant built a seven-shot, gas-seal revolver called the Nagant M1895 for the Russian Empire and chambered it for a proprietary 7.62x38R cartridge. The sturdy handgun featured an unusual gas-seal system in which the cylinder moved forward when the gun was cocked. The action closed the gap between the cylinder and the barrel, providing a boost to the muzzle velocity of the fired projectile. Nagant's M1895 became the standard issue sidearm for Russian, and later Soviet, army and law enforcement officers. The gun was used in great numbers in World War II, only to be fully replaced in 1952 by the Makarov pistol. The Nagant revolver's sealed firing system meant that, unlike most revolvers, sound suppressors could be effectively fitted to it.

A fine, though little-known brand of double-action revolvers introduced in the early 1880s, such as its Pocket Army, were the guns of Merwin, Hulbert and Co. It has been written, perhaps apocryphally, that the quality of machining was so precise that the act of opening and closing for loading and unloading created a vacuum that caused the guns to draw themselves part-way closed. In .38 caliber the revolvers were five-shot, but in .32 they were seven-shot.

Revolver Design, 21st-Century Style. Before the turn of the 20th century, John Browning and many others—including his father, Jonathan, who built the "harmonica gun"—were working on pistol designs that would hold more rounds and load faster than conventional six-shooters. Their work ultimately led to the modern semi-automatic. The flat profile of 1911-style pistols was more suitable for concealed carry and although it took the better part of a century, semi-autos have largely replaced revolvers in military and law enforcement use (in military use, beginning about 1910; in law enforcement, generally in the 1980s).

Revolvers are still popular, however, as back-up and off-duty guns among American law enforcement officers and security guards. Today's precision-machined revolver has the attraction of being a fairly simple, nothing-can-go-wrong firearm.

The 20th century was an era of firepower during which significant weapon designs continued to be developed. Smith and Wesson's contribution to cartridge development was the first magnum revolver, the .357 Magnum, which the company introduced in 1935.

The .357 Magnum cartridge was created by Elmer Keith, Phillip Sharpe, and D.B. Wesson and it is a great example of a cartridge creating a gun. It was based on Smith and Wesson's .38 Special and is credited with starting the magnum era of handgun shooting. The impetus was competition with Colt's .38 Super cartridge, which could penetrate automobile doors and defeat the bullet-proof vests of the day. In terms of stopping power, the .357 is still regarded as an excellent self-defense round.

The double-action Colt Python in .357 Magnum was introduced in 1955 and the Sturm, Ruger GP100 as late as 1986. The Python was produced and discontinued more than once, but Ruger's .357 is still in production.

Smith and Wesson introduced its .44 Magnum Model 29 in 1956. It became famous when, in the 1983 movie *Sudden Impact*, Clint Eastwood uttered the popular throw-away line "Go ahead. Make my day." Nine years later, the company marketed the Model 60, the world's first stainless steel revolver.

Today's Revolver. Why shoot a revolver when a modern semi-automatic carries more rounds, reloads faster, is flatter and slimmer, and is no more costly?

Revolvers are no-problem guns. With a relatively straightforward design, a revolver is reliable. A semi-automatic is sensitive to cartridges, and stories about jammed actions because of insufficiently powerful rounds are numerous. Revolvers do not jam. If a revolver misfires or a case is underpowered, the shooter simply pulls the trigger again.

The complexity of a semi-auto's mechanics compared to a revolver gives the revolver an edge in durability. A revolver can take a great deal of punishment and still shoot a tight group.

The final point in favor of revolvers is their ability to accept powerful loads. No semi-autos can withstand the power of loads such as .454 Casull or .475 Linebaugh.

In short, revolvers still rock!

BERETTA LARAMIE
.38 S&W Special

BERETTA STAMPEDE MARSHALL OLD WEST
.45 Colt

CHARTER ARMS BULLDOG
.44 S&W Special

CHARTER ARMS PATHFINDER
.22 LR

CHARTER ARMS PINK LADY
.38 S&W Special +P

CHARTER ARMS TARGET MAG PUG
.357 S&W Mag.

CHARTER ARMS UNDERCOVER
.38 S&W Special +P

CHARTER ARMS UNDERCOVER LITE
.38 S&W Special +P

CHIAPPA MODEL 1873-22
.22 LR

CHIAPPA RHINO 50DS
.357 S&W Mag.

CHIAPPA RHINO 2"
.357 S&W Mag.

COLT NEW FRONTIER
.44 Special

COLT P1841 SA ARMY
.357 Mag.

COLT P1850 SA ARMY
.45 LC

EUROPEAN AMERICAN ARMORY BOUNTY HUNTER
.45 LC

EUROPEAN AMERICAN ARMORY WINDICATOR
.38 Special/.357 S&W Mag.

HERITAGE MANUFACTURING BIG BORE
.45 LC

HERITAGE MANUFACTURING SMALL BORE
.22 LR

HERITAGE MANUFACTURING SMALL BORE COMBO
.22 Mag./.22 LR

MAGNUM RESEARCH BFR
.44 Mag.

NORTH AMERICAN ARMS 22 LONG RIFLE
.22 LR

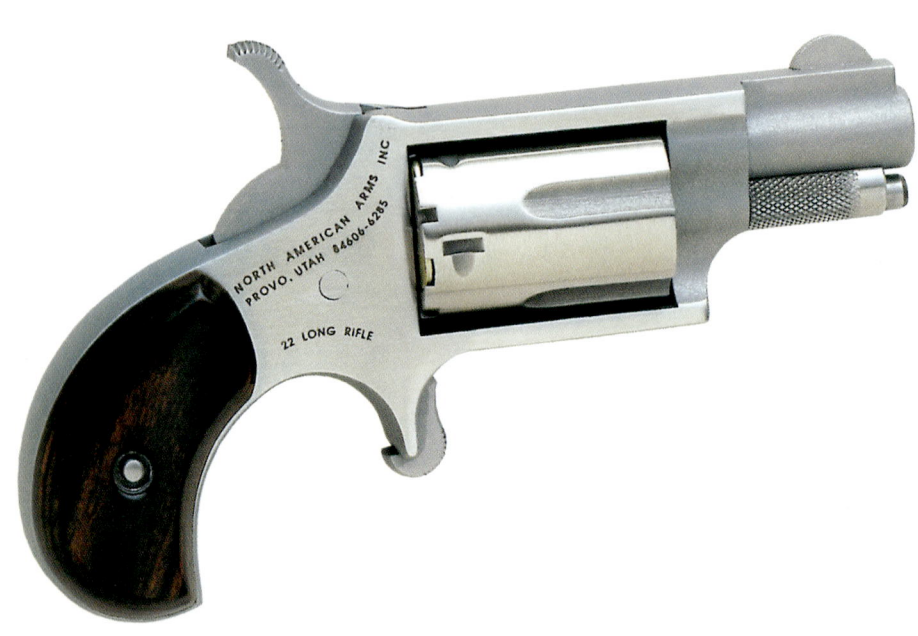

NORTH AMERICAN ARMS PUG TRITIUM
.22 WMR

Model #: NAA-Pug-T
NAA PUG Tritium Sight

Model #: NAA-Pug-D
NAA PUG White Dot

ROSSI 97206
.357 S&W Mag.

ROSSI R35102 CENTERFIRE
.38 Special

ROSSI R85104
.38 S&W Special +P

ROSSI R98104 PLINKER
.22 LR

RUGER BEARCAT
.22 LR

RUGER BISLEY VAQUERO
.45 LC

RUGER BLACKHAWK
.357 Mag.

RUGER GP100 DOUBLE-ACTION CENTERFIRE
.357/.38 Special

RUGER LCR
.38 Special+P

RUGER NEW MODEL SINGLE SIX CONVERTIBLE
.22 LR/.22 WMR

RUGER REDHAWK
.44 Mag.

RUGER SINGLE NINE
.22 WMR

RUGER SINGLE TEN
.22 LR

RUGER SP101
.357 S&W Mag.

RUGER SUPER BLACKHAWK BISLEY HUNTER
.44 Rem. Mag.

RUGER SUPER REDHAWK
.480

RUGER VAQUERO CENTERFIRE
.45 Colt

SMITH & WESSON 10
.38 S&W Special +P

SMITH & WESSON 17 MASTERPIECE
.22 LR

SMITH & WESSON 29 - S&W CLASSICS - 4"
.44 S&W Special

SMITH & WESSON 317 J-FRAME CENTERFIRE
.22 LR

SMITH & WESSON 325 THUNDER RANCH
.45 ACP

SMITH & WESSON 340PD CENTERFIRE
.357/.38 Special

SMITH & WESSON 460XVR
.460 S&W MAG

SMITH & WESSON 500 X-FRAME CENTERFIRE
.500

SMITH & WESSON 586
.38 S&W Special +P

SMITH & WESSON 627
.357/.38 Special

SMITH & WESSON 629 OUTFITTER SERIES CENTERFIRE
.44 Mag.

SMITH & WESSON 638 AIRWEIGHT
.38 Special

SMITH & WESSON 642LS LADY SMITH
.38 Special + P

SMITH & WESSON 686 PLUS
.357/.38 Special

SMITH & WESSON 686SSR CENTERFIRE
.38 Special+P

SMITH & WESSON BODYGUARD
.38 Special +P

SMITH & WESSON GOVERNOR
.410 2-1/2" shotshells, .45 ACP, or .45 Colt ammo

SMITH & WESSON M&P R8
.357/.38 Special

TAURUS 44 TRACKER
.44 Rem. Mag.

TAURUS 65
.357 Mag.

TAURUS 66
.357 Mag.

TAURUS 85BPP2
.38 Special

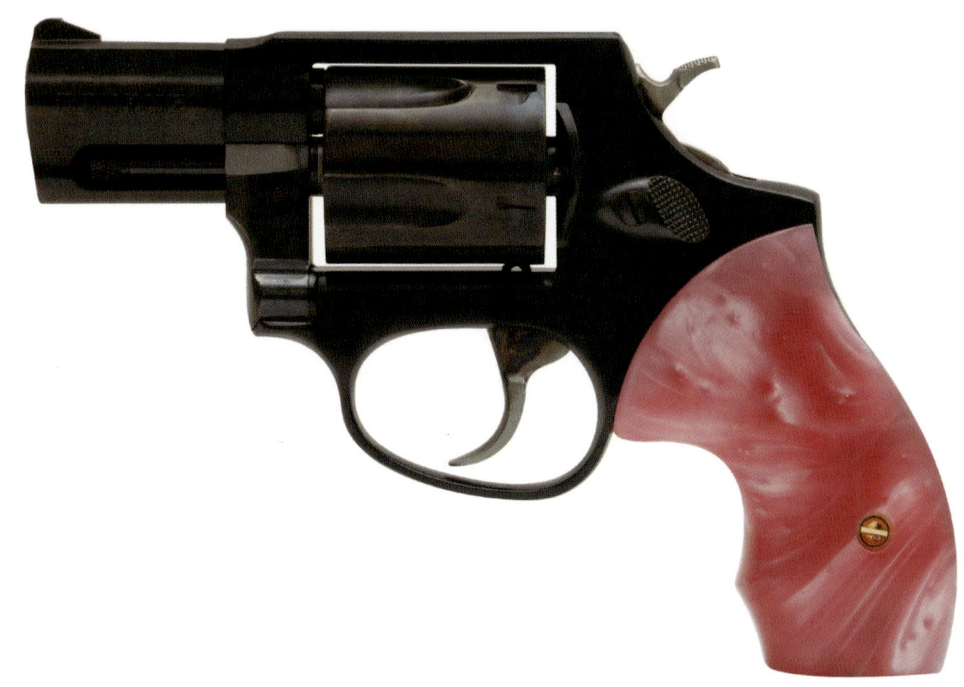

TAURUS 94
.22 S/L/LR

TAURUS 444 ULTRALITE
.44 Rem. Mag.

TAURUS 454 RAGING BULL
.454 Casull

TAURUS 608
.357 Mag.

TAURUS 627 TRACKER
.357 S&W Mag.

TAURUS 990
.22 LR

TAURUS 992 TRACKER HANDGUN COMBO
.22 Mag./.22 LR

TAURUS PUBLIC DEFENDER POLYMER
.45 LC/.410 Bore

TAURUS RAGING JUDGE M513
.45 LC/.410 Bore

TAURUS RAGING JUDGE MAGNUM
.454 Casull/.45 LC/.410 Bore

TAURUS THE JUDGE 4510
.45 LC/.410 Bore

TAURUS ULTRA-LITE, PROTECTOR 851
.38 S&W Special +P

UBERTI 1848 WHITNEYVILLE DRAGOON
.44

UBERTI 1873 CATTLEMAN
.45 LC

UBERTI 1873 CATTLEMAN 12 SHOT
.22 LR

UBERTI 1873 CATTLEMAN HOMBRE
.45 LC

UBERTI 1873 HORSEMAN
.45 LC

UBERTI 1873 STALLION BIRDSHEAD
.38 S&W Special

UBERTI 1875 ARMY OUTLAW
.45 LC

UBERTI 1875 FRONTIER
.45 LC

UBERTI 1875 TOP BREAK
.45 LC

INDEX

Beretta
Laramie	14
Stampede Marshall Old West	15

Charter Arms
Bulldog	16
Pathfinder	17
Pink Lady	18
Target Mag Pug	19
Undercover	20
Undercover Lite	21

Chiappa
Model 1873-22	22
Rhino 50DS	23
Rhino 2"	24

Colt
New Frontier	25
P1841 SA Army	26
P1850 SA Army	27

European American Armory
Bounty Hunter	28
Windicator	29

Heritage Manufacturing
Big Bore	30
Small Bore	31
Small Bore Combo	32

Magnum Research
BFR	33

North American Arms
22 Long Rifle	34
PUG Tritium	35

Rossi
97206	36
R35102 Centerfire	37
R85104	38
R98104 "Plinker"	39

Ruger
Bearcat	40
Bisley Vaquero	41
Blackhawk	42
GP100 Double-Action Centerfire	43
LCR	44
New Model Single Six Convertible	45
Redhawk	46
Single-Nine	47
Single Ten	48
SP10	49
Super Blackhawk Bisley Hunter	50
Super Redhawk	51
Vaquero Centerfire	52

Smith & Wesson
10	53
17 Masterpiece	54
29 - S&W Classics - 4"	55
317 J-Frame Centerfire	56
325 Thunder Ranch	57
340PD Centerfire	58
460XVR	59
500 X-Frame Centerfire	60
586	61
627	62
629 Outfitter Series Centerfire	63
638 Airweight	64
642LS Lady Smith	65
686 Plus	66
686SSR Centerfire	67
Bodyguard	68
Governor	69
M&P R8	70

Taurus
44 Tracker	71
65	72
66	73
85BPP2	74
94	75
444 Ultralite	76
454 Raging Bull	77
608	78
627 Tracker	79
990	80
992 Tracker Handgun Combo	81
Public Defender Polymer	82
Raging Judge M513	83
Raging Judge Magnum	84
The Judge 4510	85
Ultra-Lite, Protector 851	86

Uberti
1848 Whitneyville Dragoon	87
1873 Cattleman	88
1873 Cattleman 12 Shot	89
1873 Cattleman Hombre	90
1873 Horseman	91
1873 Stallion Birdshead	92
1875 Army Outlaw	93
1875 Frontier	94
1875 Top Break	95